Who Was Vince Lombardi?

By Tracy Cronce
Illustrated by Paul Cooper
Cover Illustration by Sadie Cronce

Vince at the dedication of Lombardi Avenue, in Green Bay,
Wisconsin in 1968

"Most times streets are named after the deceased,
I hope this is not...

I just want you to know I'm not dead."

~Vince Lombardi

Beckham Publications

USA

DEDICATION

To my human and canine family. Love you all.-TC

To all my critters. -SC

To Rebee Tebe. -PC

A statue of Vince Lombardi that stands outside Lambeau Field, in Green Bay, Wisconsin

"It's not whether you get knocked down, it's whether you get up."

~Vince Lombardi

CONTENTS

Who Was Vince Lombardi 16

Growing Up Lombardi 28

Coaching Jobs for Vince 45

The New York Giants 56

Lombardi Goes to Green Bay 60

Continuing Success 73

More About Vince 103

Timeline 117

Bibliography 120

Green Bay Packers quarterback, Bart Starr

"Winning is not everything, it's the only thing. In our business there is no second place."

~Vince Lombardi

...

Later, Vince was quoted as saying,

"I wish I had never said that. What I believe is: If you go out on a football field or any other endeavor in life and you leave every fiber of what you have on that field, when the game finally ends, then you've won, and to me that tells more than the final score, and I never made that clear."

FOOTBALL EQUIPMENT THROUGH THE YEARS

CLEATS: CLEATS ARE SHOES THAT HAVE PEGS ON THE BOTTOM. THEY STARTED OUT BEING MADE OF WOOD OR METAL AND WERE USED MAINLY BY SOCCER PLAYERS. LATER THE PEGS WERE MADE SO THEY COULD BE REMOVED AND WERE RUBBER. TODAY, CLEATS ARE LIGHTWEIGHT AND ABLE TO STAND UP TO MUDDY AND SNOWY FIELDS.

FOOTBALL HELMETS: HELMETS HAVE ONLY BEEN REQUIRED FOR FOOTBALL PLAYERS SINCE 1943. THE FIRST HELMETS WERE MADE OF MOLESKIN. LATER SOME PADDING WAS ADDED TO HELP CUSHION THE HEAD WHEN IT WAS HIT. EAR HOLES WERE

ALSO ADDED TO ALLOW THE PLAYERS TO HEAR THE CALLS ON THE FIELD. IN 1940, THE RIDDELL COMPANY DEVELOPED PLASTIC HELMETS. THE FIRST PLASTIC HELMETS WOULD SOMETIMES SHATTER WHEN HIT, SO RIDDELL HAD TO GO BACK AND MAKE SOME CHANGES. THE CLEVELAND BROWNS COACH INVENTED THE SINGLE BAR FACE MASK IN 1953, AND THE RADIO HELMET IN 1955. AFTER THREE GAMES, THE RADIO HELMET WAS BANNED AND REMAINED BANNED UNTIL 1994. NOW, HELMETS ARE SO SMART THAT THEY CAN MEASURE HOW HARD A PLAYER HAS BEEN HIT. THIS HELPS PLAYERS AVOID CONCUSSIONS. PERHAPS IT WOULD BE GOOD TO REQUIRE PADDING ON

THE OUTSIDE OF THE HELMET TO HELP PROTECT THE PLAYER INSIDE, AS WELL AS THE PLAYER BEING SLAMMED BY THE HELMETED PLAYER.

FOOTBALL: THE BALL MUST BE A WILSON FOOTBALL WITH THE COMMISSIONER'S SIGNATURE ON IT. IT MUST BE INFLATED BETWEEN 12.5 AND 13.5 POUNDS. IT ALSO HAS TO BE TAN IN COLOR. THE REFEREE GETS TO MAKE THE FINAL DECISION WHETHER THE FOOTBALL IS OF LEGAL SIZE AND SHAPE.

Football shoes with wooden pegs pictured above

WHO WAS VINCE LOMBARDI?

Vince Lombardi always loved to watch sports. He especially loved football. As a child, Vince often organized football matches with the kids in his neighborhood and his cousins. Vince had over 51 cousins!

When Vince grew up, he would be a head coach of a football team. Not just any football team, but the Green Bay Packers. Vince felt the Packers could do great things for the NFL. What great things?

Win championships.

Today, Lombardi's Green Bay Packers are known for winning five championships including the first two Super Bowls. Before Vince took over coaching the team, few thought the Packers were a great team.

Professional football began in 1919. When Vince was a kid, most people enjoyed watching college football. Professional teams didn't have many people watching at that time and attendance at games was low.

Small towns across the USA had teams joining the NFL and then dropping out. Teams were moved from one city to the next. The only team that <u>never</u> changed cities in the NFL was the Green Bay Packers.

Then, in 1955, CBS signed a contract with the NFL to start showing the games on television. Because of this, people started going to professional football games.

The Green Bay Packers began in 1919 and became a professional team in 1921. Their success varied by year, but they did have a time from 1929-1944 where they finished either first or second in the league and won six championship games. From 1944-1958, the Packers began to struggle. Their head coach often changed and the coaching style varied. From 1950-1958, the head coach of the Packers changed six times. Wisconsin fans were beginning to lose heart in ever winning a championship again. The fans were frustrated. The players were seen as sloppy, often wearing jeans and t-shirts on game day. They were also seen out late at night right before a game, which meant they weren't getting the rest they needed for the game. The team lacked leadership and discipline. Vince was going to change that. He knew a lot about leadership and discipline. The first day of training camp Vince said to his players, "I've never been a losing coach and I don't intend to start here."

Vince had a plan to lead the Packers on to become a winning team once again.

Vince Lombardi with two Green Bay Packers

DIVISIONS OF THE NFL

THE NFL IS DIVIDED INTO TWO LEAGUES: THE AFC (AMERICAN FOOTBALL CONFERENCE), AND THE NFC (NATIONAL FOOTBALL CONFERENCE). IN THE 1960S, WHEN VINCE LOMBARDI WAS THE COACH OF THE PACKERS, THESE TWO LEAGUES WEREN'T CONNECTED TO EACH OTHER. ON JUNE 8, 1966, THE TWO LEAGUES JOINED TO FORM THE NFL (NATIONAL FOOTBALL LEAGUE). THE DIVISIONS ARE AS FOLLOWS:

AFC EAST: BUFFALO BILLS, MIAMI DOLPHINS, NEW ENGLAND PATRIOTS, NEW YORK JETS

NFC EAST: DALLAS COWBOYS, NEW YORK GIANTS, PHILADELPHIA EAGLES, WASHINGTON REDSKINS

AFC NORTH: BALTIMORE RAVENS, CINCINNATI BENGALS, CLEVELAND BROWN, PITTSBURGH STEELERS

NFC NORTH: CHICAGO BEARS, DETROIT LIONS, GREEN BAY PACKERS, MINNESOTA VIKINGS

AFC SOUTH: HOUSTON TEXANS, INDIANAPOLIS COLTS, JACKSONVILLE JAGUARS, TENNESSEE TITANS

NFC SOUTH: ATLANTA FALCONS, CAROLINA PANTHERS, NEW ORLEANS SAINTS, TAMPA BAY BUCCANEERS

AFC WEST: DENVER BRONCOS, KANSAS CITY CHIEFS, LOS ANGELES CHARGERS, OAKLAND RAIDERS

NFC WEST: ARIZONA CARDINALS, LOS ANGELES RAMS, SAN FRANCISCO 49ERS, SEATTLE SEAHAWKS

WHO OWNS THE GREEN BAY PACKERS?

THE GREEN BAY PACKERS ARE THE ONLY TEAM IN THE NFL THAT ARE OWNED BY 112,000 PEOPLE. FANS OWN THE GREEN BAY PACKERS. IN 1923, THE PACKERS WERE IN DANGER OF BECOMING BANKRUPT (UNABLE TO PAY BACK THE MONEY THEY OWE). TO SAVE THE PACKERS, THEY SOLD SHARES (PART OWNERSHIP OF THE TEAM) FOR A FEW DOLLARS EACH. THE PACKERS HAVE A BOARD OF DIRECTORS, BUT THE GENERAL MANAGER, IN ADDITION TO THE HEAD COACH, MAKES THE FOOTBALL DECISIONS. VOLUNTEERS WORK AT CONCESSION STANDS AND EVEN HELP TO SHOVEL SNOW IN THE STADIUM WHEN IT

SNOWS. NO OTHER TEAM IS COMMUNITY
OWNED.

TV AND THE NFL

TELEVISION IN THE 1950S AND 1960S VERY DIFFERENT FROM WHAT WE WATCH TODAY. BEFORE THE 1950S, TELEVISION SHOWS WERE RECORDED LIVE, USUALLY IN NEW YORK CITY, AND PUT ONTO 16 mm FILM. NEXT, IT WAS SHIPPED OUT TO STATIONS FOR BROADCAST LATER. TELEVISION SHOWS WERE MOSTLY ABOUT COOKING, SOAP OPERAS AND WRESTLING. SOME HAD CARTOONS. THERE WERE THREE NETWORKS AT THE TIME: ABC, NBC, AND CBS.

IT WASN'T UNTIL AT&T LAID COAXIAL CABLE FROM ONE COAST OF THE UNITED STATES TO THE OTHER, THAT TELEVISION

TOOK OFF. IN THE EARLY 1960S MOST
HOMES HAD BLACK AND WHITE TELEVISION
SETS MADE MOSTLY BY RCA OR ZENITH.

What TV looked like in the 1950s and 1960s

CHAPTER 1
GROWING UP LOMBARDI

Vincent Thomas Lombardi was born on June 11, 1913 in Brooklyn, New York. He was the oldest of five children born to Harry and Matilda Lombardi. Madeline, Harold, Claire, and Joe were Vince's siblings.

Vince's family was Italian, as his ancestors had emigrated from Italy between 1876 and 1930. Being Italian, in New York, Vince often felt as if others looked down on him and didn't give him the same opportunities.

Vince's family believed in hard work and getting a good education. Harry, Vince's father, was strict with him and yelled a lot. Harry often told Vince that, "Before you can do what you do, before you exist as an individual, the first thing you have to accept is duty, the second thing is respect for authority, and the third is to develop a strong mental discipline". Vince never forgot that.

Vince's mother, Matilda, was a soft-spoken person who worked hard to keep the family home neat and clean. She was an excellent cook.

Vince looked out for his brothers and sisters. Once, when someone called the Lombardi family names for being Italian,

Vince beat up the boy. Vince, like his father, was known to have a temper. Vince even got angry if he lost his favorite card game, Hearts.

St. Mark's Catholic Church was the center of the Lombardi family's activities. Vince and his father attended mass daily. Going to mass every day was something Vince would try to do for his entire life. Vince also served as an altar boy, often getting to carry the cross.

Vince serving as an altar boy

In high school, Vince played basketball and baseball. Vince attended Cathedral Prep, which was a Catholic high school for boys who wanted to become priests. Sports was very much enjoyed by Vince. During his senior year, Vince changed schools so he was able to play football. He proved to be an excellent tackler and usually attacked players head-on, in a bull-like fashion. Vince also enjoyed learning a foreign language. He took two years of Greek.

In 1933, Vince applied for a football scholarship at Fordham University (a private Catholic college) in the Bronx, New York. He had decided against becoming a priest. Even though Vince only weighed 170 pounds, his high school coach told the Fordham football coach that Vince was 185 pounds to better his chances of getting in. Vince was accepted.

Vince studied hard every night in his dorm room. Father Mulqueen, the Dean of students, didn't take well to his college students acting out or coming in late. When he saw his students misbehaving, he would paddle them on the rear end with a drumstick. Vince made it a point to never be caught staying out late.

Vince's football coach at Fordham University was Jim Crowley. Jim grew up in Green Bay, Wisconsin and played high school football under Earl (Curly) Lambeau, one of the founders of the Green Bay Packers. As much as Vince would've liked to, he didn't get to play much football. Rather, he warmed the bench watching others play. Finally, during his senior year he was able to play both offense and defense and was one of the famous "Seven Blocks of Granite" on the team. Vince suffered several injuries. One was to his abdomen from being hit head on by another player. Another injury was to his mouth. Both injuries were hard to recover from.

While at Fordham, Vince met his future wife, Marie Planitz, who was in training to become a nurse. Vince and Marie dated steadily during college.

Vince was known by other students to be kind, caring, nice and quiet, but he had a big temper as well. His anger often frightened others and it took him a long time to learn how to control it. Saying he was sorry was a lesson he had to learn.

Vince graduated in the top 25% of his class, and the top 10% of all football players on his team.

After graduation, Vince lived at home. While looking for a job, Vince worked odd jobs. Finally, a job opportunity came.

Vince at Fordham University

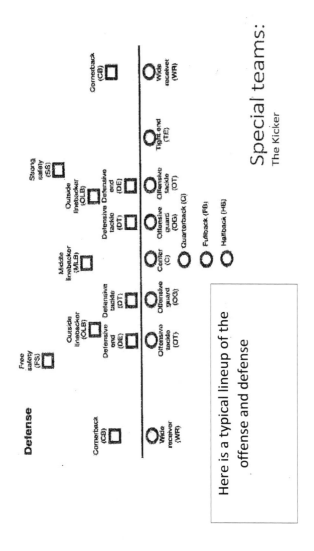

Defense

Free safety (FS)

Strong safety (SS)

Cornerback (CB)

Cornerback (CB)

Outside linebacker (OLB)

Middle linebacker (MLB)

Outside linebacker (OLB)

Defensive end (DE)

Defensive tackle (DT)

Defensive tackle (DT)

Defensive end (DE)

Wide receiver (WR)

Offensive tackle (OT)

Offensive guard (OG)

Center (C)

Offensive guard (OG)

Offensive tackle (OT)

Tight end (TE)

Wide receiver (WR)

Quarterback (C)

Fullback (FB)

Halfback (HB)

Here is a typical lineup of the offense and defense

Special teams:
The Kicker

37

"After all the cheers have died down and the stadium is empty, after the headlines have been written, and after you are back in the quiet of your room and the championship ring has been placed on the dresser and after all the pomp and fanfare have faded, the enduring thing that is left is the dedication to doing with our lives the very best we can to make the world a better place in which to live."

~Vince Lombardi

IMMIGRATION

IMMIGRATION IS WHEN A PERSON MOVES FROM THEIR HOME COUNTRY TO LIVE IN ANOTHER COUNTRY. IN SOUTHERN ITALY, WHERE VINCE'S ANCESTORS WERE FROM, MANY PEOPLE HAD TO LEAVE BECAUSE THE SOIL WAS NOT GOOD ENOUGH FOR GROWING MUCH OF ANYTHING. TO AVOID STARVATION, MANY PEOPLE FROM EUROPE MOVED TO THE U.S. IN SEARCH OF A BETTER LIFE.

ELLIS ISLAND WAS OPENED IN 1892 AND WAS THE FIRST IMMIGRATION STATION TO RECEIVE IMMIGRANTS INTO THE UNITED STATES.

TIMELINE OF IMMIGRANTS COMING INTO THE
UNITED STATES:

1630-1640 ABOUT 20,000 IMMIGRANTS CAME
TO AMERICA TO GAIN RELIGIOUS FREEDOM

1680-1790 MANY AFRICANS WERE BROUGHT
TO AMERICA AGAINST THEIR WILL TO WORK
AS SLAVES.

1815-1865 NORTHERN AND WESTERN
EUROPEANS COME TO AMERICA LOOKING
FOR A BETTER LIFE FOR THEIR FAMILIES.

1880-1920 ABOUT 4 MILLION SOUTHERN,
EASTERN, AND CENTRAL EUROPEANS
ENTER THE U.S. SEEKING A BETTER LIFE.
MANY ITALIAN IMMIGRANTS SETTLED IN
BIGGER CITIES LIKE NEW YORK CITY. MANY

ITALIANS WERE TREATED AS LESS THAN EQUAL.

CURLY LAMBEAU

CURLY LAMBEAU WAS BORN IN GREEN BAY, WISCONSIN ON APRIL 9, 1898. CURLY WAS AN EXCELLENT ATHLETE IN HIGH SCHOOL AND WENT ON TO PLAY FOR NOTRE DAME.

AFTER NOTRE DAME, HE CAME BACK TO GREEN BAY TO WORK FOR THE INDIAN PACKING COMPANY. LAMBEAU AND A GREEN BAY PRESS-GAZETTE SPORTS EDITOR GEORGE WHITNEY CALHOUN, FOUNDED THE GREEN BAY PACKERS ON AUGUST 11, 1919.

LAMBEAU WAS THE HEAD COACH FROM 1920-1949. THE PACKERS WON SIX CHAMPIONSHIPS WHILE LAMBEAU WAS THE

COACH. LAMBEAU ALSO PLAYED FOR THE TEAM, SERVING AS THE TEAM'S HALFBACK, BOTH RUNNING AND PASSING. HE LATER WAS THE TEAM'S KICKER. LAMBEAU HAS THE RECORD FOR THE MOST WINS AS A GREEN BAY COACH. BECAUSE HE WAS A COACH FOR SO LONG, HE ALSO HAD THE MOST LOSSES.

LAMBEAU, WITH THE HELP OF DON HUTSON, ONE OF THE BEST RECEIVERS IN THE NFL, MADE THE PACKERS ONE OF THE STRONGEST TEAMS IN THE NFL AT THE TIME.

LAMBEAU WAS NAMED TO THE PRO-FOOTBALL HALL OF FAME IN 1963. HIS INNOVATIONS INCLUDE HAVING FOOTBALL

PLAYERS PRACTICE ON A DAILY BASIS, THE FORWARD PASS, AND TAKING AN AIRPLANE TO GET TO GAMES THAT WEREN'T AT HOME.

THE PACKERS' STADIUM IS NAMED AFTER CURLY LAMBEAU AS IS A STREET IN GREEN BAY NEAR THE STADIUM.

CHAPTER 2
COACHING JOBS FOR VINCE

After hunting for a coaching job, Vince found one in Englewood, New Jersey at St. Cecelia High School. Vince was also expected to teach! This was a big surprise, as he had never taught before.

Vince taught physics, chemistry, Latin, PE, and was the team's basketball coach, and an assistant football coach. Vince learned that he was to do all of that for a salary of $1000 a year.

Vince knew this was going to be a big task, but he didn't get discouraged. He worked hard, stayed late at work to make time for what he was interested in, being the assistant football coach.

As an assistant football coach, Vince worked mainly with the linemen. A lineman is the person who plays at the line of scrimmage. Linemen are usually the biggest players on the field. Strength is important for a lineman. There are linemen on both the offense and the defense.

As Vince started coaching football, he had to learn about each of his players. In addition, he discovered that each player needed to be coached differently. Some players needed a lot of help when it came to football, while others did better when they were left alone.

The football players also learned their new coach could get upset. When a mistake was made, Coach Lombardi could yell at you, throw things, kick a garbage can, or if he was really mad, he'd blink his eyes at you before yelling and screaming.

After eight years at St. Cecelia's, Vince accepted an assistant coaching position back at Fordham, the same school he'd gone to college at. Vince worked under head football coach Ed Danowski.

The football team at Fordham had not been practicing however, as Jim Crowley, the former head coach, had gone to serve as a Navy Commander during World War II. The football equipment got old and collected dust while Crowley was away.

Vince spent two years at Fordham University, but the team did not do well.

Then, in 1948, Vince got the opportunity to coach at West Point Military Academy. Vince interviewed three times and finally got the job! The head coach there was Colonel Earl Blaik. Everyone called him Red. Red Blaik worked his football players hard. Blaik expected the players to do well.

West Point hired Vince as an assistant coach earning $7000 per year. Although Vince would have loved to be the head coach, he felt he had some things to learn from Coach Blaik.

Vince put in long days coaching, planning, and watching films of football games to learn about what could be done to improve their chances of winning. West Point was one of the first teams to use films of past games to help improve players' skills.

On game days, Lombardi would get extremely tense and worked up. He wanted his team to win. When Vince joined West Point their record was 57 wins, 3 losses and 4 ties. Vince hoped to continue that. The team did well.

Then, in 1951, West Point had to expel 90 of their cadets because of cheating on tests in school. This was very hard on the team and losing many of the football players caused the team to not do so well for two years afterwards.

By 1953, Vince began to look for a bigger and better coaching position. He really hoped to become a head football coach. Vince had seen other assistant coaches who'd worked under Coach Blaik go on to get top coaching positions, so Vince was hopeful.

Vince as an assistant coach at West Point

"The quality of a person's life in in direct proportion to their commitment to excellence, regardless of their chosen field of endeavor."

~Vince Lombardi

WEST POINT

WEST POINT IS AN ARMY MILITARY ACADEMY THAT WAS STARTED IN 1802. STUDENTS GO THERE FOR FOUR YEARS TO ATTEND COLLEGE AFTER GRADUATION FROM HIGH SCHOOL. UPON GRADUATION, STUDENTS EARN A DEGREE AND BECOME AN OFFICER IN THE ARMY.

WEST POINT OFFERS MANY DEGREE PROGRAMS. WHILE GOING TO WEST POINT, THE STUDENTS HAVE AN OPPORTUNITY TO PLAY SPORTS.

THINK IT'S EASY TO GET INTO WEST POINT? THINK AGAIN. ONLY 9% OF STUDENTS WHO APPLY GET IN. THAT

MEANS IF 100 PEOPLE APPLY THERE, ONLY 9 WILL BE ACCEPTED. YOU NEED TO HAVE ALMOST ALL A'S ON YOUR REPORT CARD AND BE AN EXCELLENT WRITER.

WHILE AT WEST POINT, STUDENTS SPEND ABOUT TWO HOURS EVERYDAY ON DRILLS, TRAININGS, AND SPORTS. IN ADDITION, THERE ARE HOURS OF STUDYING EACH NIGHT.

WEST POINT IS A DIVISION I SCHOOL, WHICH MEANS IT IS ONE OF THE MOST COMPETITIVE AND LARGEST SCHOOLS IN THE NCAA (NATIONAL COLLEGIATE ATHLETIC ASSOCIATION).

WEST POINT'S TEAM IS CALLED THE BLACK KNIGHTS.

TODAY, THE ARMY BLACK KNIGHTS OF WEST POINT PRACTICE AND PLAY ON BLAIK FIELD, NAMED AFTER THEIR HEAD COACH EARL "RED" BLAIK.

CHAPTER 3
THE NEW YORK GIANTS

In 1954, the New York Giants had a head coaching position open. Lombardi hoped to get the job. The Giants wanted Red Blaik to be the coach, but Blaik turned down the job. Next, the Giants interviewed and hired Jim Lee Howell, a man who had once played football for the New York Giants.

In 1954 Lombardi was offered a job as an assistant coach of the New York Giants football team. Vince would coach the offense. The defensive coach was Tom Landry who later became the Cowboys head coach. Vince took the job and his pay was $14,000 per year. Working with head coach Jim Lee Howell was exciting to Vince.

Lombardi was happy to be able to work with professional football players. Vince put in even more hours than he did while with West Point. He studied the films of past games and stayed at work longer than any of the other coaches. He felt that having discipline was extremely important.

When working with the backfield players, Vince demanded that they try to be perfect in how plays were completed. Because Vince was disciplined, he thought his players should be too. Many players found Lombardi to be somewhat hard to work with and some even thought he was abusive in his treatment of them. Rookie (new) players were expected to know all the plays right away. And when they didn't, Vince got upset.

The New York Giants had only won three games the year before Vince got hired, so Lombardi was sure he could help his players do better.

The Giants did do better. They won seven games and had five losses. It was a happy time for Giants fans.

Lombardi spent five years with the New York Giants. He even turned down a head coaching job with the Philadelphia Eagles to stay in New York. The Eagles were the worst team in the National Football League at the time and had hoped to turn their team around with the help of Vince's great coaching. Vince and his family wanted to stick with the Giants a while longer and he wanted a head coaching job where he could also be the general manager.

The Giants did continue to have a winning record with the help of Lombardi.

"The difference between a successful person and others is not lack of strength, not a lack of knowledge, but rather a lack of will."

~Vince Lombardi

CHAPTER 4
LOMBARDI GOES TO GREEN BAY

The Green Bay Packers had struggled to win many games since 1945. Packer fans started getting used to losing games. Having won only one game during the 1958 season, Vince had his work cut out for him when he began as head coach in 1959.

Vince took the Green Bay Packer head-coaching job because he was also able to be the team's general manager. Being the general manager was important to Vince because it allowed him to have a say in whom the team hired and how the team operated.

When the Green Bay Packers first started playing football, their colors were blue and gold. Curly Lambeau and George Whitney Calhoun started the team. The Indian Packing Company sponsored the team. The Indian Packing Company gave $500 to start the team and buy uniforms for the players. Then in January 1921, the Acme Packing Company took over the Indian Packing Company. They became the sponsor of the Green Bay Packers. Acme's sponsorship lasted less than a year. After that, the Acme Packing Company moved to Chicago and went bankrupt. After that, they were called the

Green Bay Packers. Eventually, around 1950, the Packers colors were changed to taxicab yellow and forest green. Lombardi made some changes to the uniforms when he first started, asking the players to all wear the same style cleats and adding three stripes to the socks.

When Vince took the job in Green Bay, he was hired for $36,000.00 a year. His contract was for five years.

Vince moved his family to Green Bay, Wisconsin from New York. The change was hard on his family who was used to having a big city to shop in and many friends. When Vince, his wife Marie, and his two children, son Vince Jr. and daughter Susan rolled into town in their pink Chevrolet, Green Bay was not a big city like New York City was. The population of Green Bay at that time was around 60,000 people, much smaller than the seven million people that lived in New York City at the time.

The quarterback for the Green Bay Packers was Paul Hornung. Who was Paul Hornung? Paul had gone to college at Notre Dame, a big school in South Bend, Indiana. At the end of college, Paul won the Heisman Trophy in 1956. The Heisman Trophy is an award given to the best college football player each year. After college, the Green Bay Packers drafted Paul in the first round in 1957.

Paul's nickname was "The Golden Boy", as he was good looking.

Prior to Lombardi coming to Green Bay, Paul played different positions on the Packers team. Vince told Paul that he was going to be the key to having a successful football season. Lombardi had watched films of the Packers from past games and felt Hornung would be best as a halfback.

Training camp began with Vince telling his players that he expected no less than 100% effort at all times.   If Lombardi felt that one of his players weren't trying, he'd make them run laps around the field. Players were worked to the point of exhaustion each day. Vince's voice could be heard across the entire practice field. He was that loud!

The pre-season finished with four wins and two losses. Vince had a hard time choosing who would be his quarterback, Bart Starr or Lamar McHan. He chose McHan in the beginning. Starr was often quiet and didn't show great leadership. Having been raised by a military father, Starr needed someone like Lombardi to help him develop leadership skills. The Packers started out with three wins, but they lost the next five games. Vince decided to have Bart Starr take over as quarterback. The Packers did win the next five games to finish out their first season with seven wins and five losses. This was the first time the Packers had a winning season since 1944.

Vince with his wife Marie, daughter Susan, and

son Vince Jr.

"There are three things that are important to
every man in this locker room. His God, his
family, and the Green Bay Packers. In that order."

~Vince Lombardi

THE CITY OF GREEN BAY

A FRENCH EXPLORER NAMED JEAN

NICOLET FOUNDED THE CITY OF GREEN BAY

IN 1634. HE CALLED IT GREEN BAY BECAUSE

OF THE COLOR OF THE WATER. NICOLET SET

UP A FUR TRADING POST THERE. HE MET

NATIVE AMERICANS OF THE MENOMINEE

AND HO-CHUNK TRIBES WHO HAD A

HISTORY OF LIVING IN THE AREA FOR OVER

10,000 YEARS! THEY LIKED THE AREA

BECAUSE OF THE FISHING AND WILDLIFE

THAT LIVED THERE. THE FIRST WHITE

SETTLERS ARRIVED IN 1745. GREEN BAY IS THE THIRD LARGEST CITY IN WISCONSIN, AFTER MILWAUKEE AND MADISON.

GREEN BAY IS HOME TO THE FIRST NEWSPAPER IN THE STATE, WHICH WAS CALLED, "THE INTELLIGENCER", STARTED IN 1833.

WHEN VINCE ANNOUNCED TO HIS FAMILY THAT THEY WERE MOVING TO GREEN BAY, WISCONSIN, HIS DAUGHTER SUSAN SAID, "WHERE'S WISCONSIN?" VINCE GOT OUT A MAP AND SHOWED HER WHERE WISCONSIN WAS, BUT HE COULDN'T FIND GREEN BAY ON THE MAP. THEN, SUSAN SAID, "WELL I'M NOT MOVING ANYPLACE THAT'S NOT ON THE MAP."

VINCE TOLD SUSAN, "WHEN I AM DONE, IT WILL BE ON THAT MAP, AND YOU'LL KNOW EXACTLY, SUSAN, WHERE YOU LIVED."

The population of Green Bay, Wisconsin in 1959

"Winning is not everything-but making the effort to win is."

~Vince Lombardi

LAMBEAU FIELD

LAMBEAU FIELD DIDN'T START OUT WITH THE NAME LAMBEAU FIELD. IT WAS ORIGINALLY CALLED NEW CITY STADIUM AND WAS BUILT IN 1957 IN GREEN BAY, WISCONSIN AFTER THE PACKERS STOPPED USING EAST HIGH SCHOOL'S FIELD. IN AUGUST OF 1965, PACKER'S FOUNDER, CURLY LAMBEAU PASSED AWAY AND THE FIELD WAS RE-NAMED TO HONOR HIS MEMORY. THE STREET THE FIELD SITS ON

WAS ONCE CALLED HIGHLAND AVENUE BUT WAS CHANGED TO LOMBARDI AVENUE IN 1968, TO HONOR VINCE LOMBARDI. THE STADIUM COST $960,000.00 AND THE FIELD HELD ABOUT 32,000 PEOPLE UNTIL 2013 WHEN THE STADIUM ADDED 7000 SEATS. THIS EXPANSION COST $140 MILLION DOLLARS. LAMBEAU FIELD IS THE OLDEST FIELD IN OPERATION IN THE NFL.

CHAPTER 5
CONTINUING SUCCESS

Before the start of his second season with the Packers, the New York Giants tried to get Vince to come back to take over as head coach. Vince asked New York to give him one more year in Green Bay, as the team wasn't ready to give him up as their head coach. The Packers gave Vince a $10,000.00 bonus since his first year had gone so well. In addition, Lombardi was chosen as Professional Coach of the Year.

In 1960, professional football was just beginning to be shown on television. This allowed people to watch from their homes. The field was the perfect shape and size to fit on a television screen.

At the start of Vince's second season with Green Bay, he had a difficult choice between McHan and Starr for his starting quarterback. Starr was chosen. That season the Baltimore Colts tied with the Packers for first place. The winner would be decided with two games both played on the west coast of the United States.

The Green Bay Packers went to Palo Alto, California to practice. They wanted to be able to practice in privacy. Security was tight during practices and Vince didn't want any photographers in to see what they were doing. One photographer did sneak in and Vince caught him and took his camera.

The Packers did win the conference games and were now set to battle it out with the Philadelphia Eagles. The winner of this game would be the world champion.

The two teams met on December 26, 1960. It was a close game, but the Eagles won the championship 17-13. Vince didn't get angry at his players, he simply told them that while he was coach, another championship game would not be lost. Green Bay was still proud of their Packers and looked forward to another season.

The team began the 1961 season with undefeated preseason games. However, President John F. Kennedy ordered more

American troops (soldiers) to help fight in the Vietnam War. Three Packer players, Paul Hornung, Ray Nitschke, and Boyd Dowler were all called to active duty in the military during this time. They were allowed to play in Sunday football games, however. All three of them were able to play in most games, but Hornung missed two games. The Packers had an awesome season and won the championship game against Lombardi's old team, the New York Giants.

At the end of the season, President John Kennedy tried to convince Vince to return to his old team, West Point, to be the head coach. Vince decided to stay in Green Bay.

In 1962, the Packers were being noticed from people all over America. The players and team were in many magazines, including Time, Life, Look, The Saturday Evening Post, The New Yorker, The Holiday Magazine, Esquire, Sport, and Sports Illustrated. Lombardi told his players not to get a big head about becoming so popular. He worried that they would become overly confident and not try as hard.

Green Bay had a strong 1962 season, winning 13 games and only losing one! Once again, the championship game was against the New York Giants. The day started out very windy. The Packers didn't mind the wind because they ran the ball rather than passed it. The Giants, on the other hand, were passers, and the wind made it difficult for their team to get a good pass off. The Packers won 16-7. This win had Vince thinking about winning the championship game in 1963 already. If his team could win three straight championships in a row, they'd be the first NFL team to ever do that.

Lombardi was asked to be a co-author of a book called, "Run to Daylight: Vince Lombardi's Diary of One Week with the Green Bay Packers". In this book, a journalist wrote about what practice, coaching, winning and family was like for Vince Lombardi.

The 1963 championship win was not to be for the Packers, however, as Paul Hornung, one of the great players on the team, got in trouble for betting on NFL teams and was suspended from playing football. Vince was so upset that he almost quit. The Packers still had a winning season, winning 11 games, losing two, and tying one.

In 1964, the Packers continued to be successful and finished second place, tied with the Vikings with a record of 8-5-1. Vince was often moody and hard on his players and any press that wanted to interview him.

The 1965 season saw the Packers finish first in their division with a record of 10-3-

1. The also won the championship against the Browns with a score of 23-12.

Once again, in 1966, the Packers had a winning season with a 12-2 record. They took first in their division and won the NFL Championship game against the Cowboys. This was also the year that the first Super Bowl was to be played and the Packers were to play the Chiefs. The game was set for January 15, 1967 at Los Angeles Memorial Coliseum in California.

Prior to the first Super Bowl, Frank Gifford, a reporter, who had played football for the New York Giants at one time, interviewed Vince.   Frank noticed that Vince was shaking, he was so nervous. The Packer players were very nervous before the game and so Vince gave them a lot of encouragement. The final score was Packers 35, Chiefs 10. It was a big victory for the Green Bay Packers.

After winning the first Super Bowl, rumors of Lombardi retiring were being spread. Vince told everyone that it wasn't true, he was going to stick with his Packers.

The 1967 fall season began with some people saying that the Packers' players were getting too old to have another good season and probably could not win another championship. They did have a strong season, however and ended with a 9-4-1 record. The toughest loss came when the

Packers played the Los Angeles Rams. The game ended with the Rams scoring 27 and the Packers scoring a close 24 points. Lombardi took it very hard and was determined not to let that happen again. When the Packers met up for a second time against the Rams, they were ready!

They beat the Rams 28 to 7. It was a huge victory, but Lombardi didn't want his players to get too confident for the upcoming championship game against the Cowboys.

The Packers-Cowboys game started out with bitter cold temperatures in Green Bay, -20 degrees (-46 with the wind chill)! Lambeau Field froze and became rock solid. The cold was tough on the Dallas,

Texas team, and the Packers took the victory, winning 21 to 17. The game later became known as the Ice Bowl. Now the Packers were once again heading to another Super Bowl to take on the Oakland Raiders from California.

On January 14, 1968 the two teams met in Miami, Florida. The Packers led in points throughout the entire game and won 33 to 14. Quarterback Bart Starr was once again named MVP of the game. It was a great victory for everyone, but Vince was tired. He'd been talking to his family about retiring and he knew that now was the time.

Vince stepped down as head coach of the Green Bay Packers but stayed in Green

Bay to do the General Manager job. During this time, Vince enjoyed golfing and more time at home. At times he was frustrated not being able to help the new head coach, Phil Bengston, whom he'd chosen, do his job. Phil had been Lombardi's assistant coach at Green Bay.

At the end of his first year in retirement, Vince was offered a position with the Washington Redskins. The Packers weren't happy about letting Vince go, but they did.

The Redskins hadn't won a championship since 1942 and they were one of the worst teams in the NFL. He felt the challenge of transforming the team would be good for him, so he took it.

Lombardi helped to turn the Redskins losing seasons around. For the first time, the team finished with a winning record, although they didn't make the championships, fans were thrilled about having a better season. Vince, too, was excited about the changes being made and he looked forward to working with them for another season. The next season, however, didn't come, as Vince Lombardi was diagnosed with cancer.

Vince Lombardi passed away on September 3, 1970. His funeral was held back in his home state of New York. Many of his former students and players came to his funeral and spoke of how much Vince had changed their lives for the better.

Green Bay Packer kicker Mason Crosby, #2

THE KICKER-THE UNSUNG HERO

THE KICKER SCORES ABOUT 30% OF THE POINTS IN THE NFL WITH THE POINT AFTER AND THE FIELD GOALS. THE ALL-TIME SCORING LEADER BY A GREEN BAY PACKER GOES TO MASON CROSBY, A KICKER WITH 1345 POINTS. DID YOU KNOW THE LONGEST FIELD GOAL IN THE NFL WAS A 64 YARD KICK? ONLY 18 NFL PLAYERS HAVE KICKED FIELD GOALS OF 60 YARDS OR MORE.

"Winning is a habit. Watch your thoughts, they become your beliefs. Watch your beliefs, they become your words. Watch your words, they become your actions. Watch your actions, they become your habits. Watch your habits, they become your character."

~Vince Lombardi

MILWAUKEE COUNTY STADIUM

THE GREEN BAY PACKERS PLAYED TWO TO FOUR HOME GAMES A YEAR IN MILWAUKEE, WISCONSIN AT THE MILWAUKEE COUNTY STADIUM, DURING THE YEARS 1953 TO 1994. THEY ALSO USED THE STADIUM IN MILWAUKEE FOR AT LEAST ONE PRE-SEASON GAME EACH YEAR.

THE MINNESOTA VIKINGS VISITED THE PACKERS AT MILWAUKEE COUNTY STADIUM MORE THAN ANY OTHER OPPONENT.

MILWAUKEE HAD HOPES OF GETTING THE GREEN BAY PACKERS TO RELOCATE TO MILWAUKEE RATHER THAN STAYING IN GREEN BAY. HAVING THE PACKERS PLAY IN

MILWAUKEE HELPED THE CITY TO EARN OVER SIX MILLION DOLLARS FROM SELLING PACKERS RELATED MATERIALS. IF THEY HAD MOVED, WOULD THEY HAVE BEEN CALLED THE MILWAUKEE PACKERS?

THE STADIUM THE PACKERS USED IN GREEN BAY WAS CALLED THE NEW CITY STADIUM AND WAS HALF THE SIZE OF THE MILWAUKEE STADIUM. RATHER THAN MOVE TO MILWAUKEE, THE PACKERS CHOSE TO STAY IN GREEN BAY AND BUILD THEIR OWN BIGGER FIELD. THE FIELD WAS CALLED LAMBEAU FIELD AFTER THE MAN WHO STARTED THE PACKERS, CURLY LAMBEAU.

THE LOMBARDI SWEEP

VINCE WAS KNOWN FOR A PLAY FOR THE OFFENSE CALLED THE POWER SWEEP. VINCE WAS QUOTED AS SAYING, "YOU THINK THERE'S ANYTHING SPECIAL ABOUT THIS SWEEP? WELL, THERE ISN'T. IT'S A BASIC PLAY AS THERE CAN BE IN FOOTBALL. WE SIMPLY DO IT OVER AND OVER AND OVER. THERE CAN NEVER BE ENOUGH EMPHASIS ON REPETITION. I WANT MY PLAYERS TO BE ABLE TO RUN THIS SWEEP IN THEIR SLEEP. IF WE CALL THE SWEEP TWENTY TIMES, I'LL EXPECT IT TO WORK TWENTY TIMES...NOT EIGHTEEN, NOT NINETEEN."

A POWER SWEEP ALLOWED THE CENTER, THE GUY WHO SNAPS THE BALL TO THE QUARTERBACK, TO DECIDE WHICH WAY THE RUNNING BACKS ARE GOING TO RUN. THE OFFENSIVE PLAYER WHO HAS THE BALL (USUALLY THE HALF BACK OR FULL BACK) RUNS TO THE OUTSIDE OF THE RIGHT OR LEFT TACKLES. THE OTHER PLAYERS BLOCK THE DEFENSE AND ALLOW THE BACK TO RUN THROUGH WITH THE BALL.

LOMBARDI LIKED TO USE FULLBACK JIM TAYLOR OR HALF BACK PAUL HORNUNG TO RUN WITH THE BALL WHEN A SWEEP PLAY WAS CALLED. THE GUARDS JERRY KRAMER AND FUZZY THURSTON LOVED THE SWEEP BECAUSE THEIR BLOCKS GAVE THEM A

CHANCE TO SHINE. THEY CLEARED THE WAY FOR THE BACKS TO RUN TO DAYLIGHT WHEREVER THE DEFENDERS WEREN'T. THE DEFENSIVE PLAYERS' EYES BULGED OUT WHEN THEY SAW THE SWEEP COMING, BUT THERE WAS LITTLE THEY COULD DO TO STOP IT FROM GAINING YARDAGE. VINCE LEARNED ABOUT THE SWEEP PLAY WHILE AT FORDHAM WHEN HE PLAYED FOOTBALL AGAINST THE UNIVERSITY OF PITTSBURGH. VINCE TOLD THE PACKERS THAT IF THEY COULD WORK TOGETHER, THEY WOULD BECOME GREAT AT USING THIS PLAY AGAINST THEIR OPPONENTS. LOMBARDI MADE THE PLAYERS PRACTICE THE SWEEP SO OFTEN THAT THEY KNEW IT BY HEART.

GREEN BAY BECAME EXPERTS AT THE PLAY, AND THEY WON MANY GAMES BECAUSE OF PRACTICING IT AND USING IT EFFECTIVELY DURING GAMES.

Vince teaching the Lombardi Sweep to his players

SUPER BOWL I

THE FIRST SUPER BOWL WAS PLAYED JANUARY 15, 1967. THE GREEN BAY PACKERS PLAYED THE KANSAS CITY CHIEFS IN LOS ANGELES. THE PACKERS WON 35-10. THE CHIEFS WERE PART OF THE AFL (AMERICAN FOOTBALL LEAGUE) WHICH WAS ONLY STARTED IN 1960. THE PACKERS WERE PART OF THE NFL (NATIONAL FOOTBALL LEAGUE). THE TWO DIVISIONS MERGED IN 1966 AND THE OVERALL BEST TEAM WOULD BE DECIDED BY HAVING THE TWO TOP TEAMS PLAY EACH OTHER.

THE SUPER BOWL WAS ORIGINALLY CALLED THE AFL-NFL CHAMPIONSHIP GAME. IT WASN'T UNTIL LAMAR HUNT JOKED THAT

IT COULD BE CALLED THE SUPER BOWL
WHEN HE SAW TWO KIDS PLAYING WITH A
SUPER BALL. TICKETS TO THE FIRST SUPER
BOWL COST $12. THE UNIVERSITY OF
ARIZONA MARCHING BAND AND A FAMOUS
TRUMPETER WAS THE FEATURED
ENTERTAINMENT. BART STARR WAS THE
MVP OF BOTH SUPER BOWL I AND II.

THE ICE BOWL (NFL CHAMPIONSHIP GAME)

ON DECEMBER 31, 1967 THE DALLAS COWBOYS CAME TO GREEN BAY TO PLAY IN THE CHAMPIONSHIP GAME. THE DAY STARTED OUT WITH BITTER COLD TEMPERATURES OF 20 BELOW ZERO, WITH A WIND CHILL OF 46 DEGREES BELOW ZERO. THE BAND THAT WAS SUPPOSED TO PLAY WAS CANCELLED, AND THE REFEREES HAD TO USE HAND SIGNALS INSTEAD OF WHISTLES BECAUSE ONE REFEREE HAD HIS WHISTLE FROZEN TO HIS LIPS. COFFEE FROZE IN THE CUP IN LESS THAN ONE MINUTE.

NEARLY 50,000 FANS SHOWED TO WATCH THE GAME DESPITE THE TERRIBLY COLD TEMPERATURES. VINCE HAD SPENT $80,000.00 TO HAVE AN ELECTRICAL SYSTEM INSTALLED THAT WOULD HEAT THE FIELD TO AVOID IT FROM FREEZING SOLID. WITH THE COLD, THE FIELD WAS COVERED AND THE HEATING SYSTEM WAS TURNED ON. ON GAME DAY WHEN THE FIELD WAS UNCOVERED, THE FIELD FROZE SOLID WHEN THE WARM STEAM CONDENSATION ROSE UP FROM THE HEATING ELEMENT. PLAYERS NOW HAD TO TRY TO PLAY FOOTBALL ON AN ICE RINK.

RIGHT AT THE START OF THE GAME, GREEN BAY TOOK A 14-0 LEAD. IT WASN'T

UNTIL THE SECOND QUARTER THAT THE COWBOYS BEGAN TO CATCH UP WITH A 14-10 SCORE. THEN, IN THE THIRD QUARTER, THE COWBOYS TOOK A 17-14 LEAD WITH A TOUCHDOWN PASS.

AFTER DANNY ANDERSON FAILED TO MAKE IT TO THE END ZONE TWICE DUE TO SLIPPING ON THE ICE, THE PACKERS WERE LEFT WITH 16 SECONDS IN THE GAME. NO TIME OUTS REMAINED. WITH GOOD BLOCKS BY RIGHT GUARD JERRY KRAMER AND KEN BOWMAN, BART STARR PLUNGED ACROSS THE GOAL LINE FOR A TOUCH DOWN. PACKERS WON WITH A FINAL SCORE OF 21-17. WITH THIS WIN, THE PACKERS ADVANCED TO SUPER BOWL II.

Green Bay Packers scoring the final touchdown against the Dallas Cowboys during the Ice Bowl

Vince being carried off the field by two Green Bay Packers
after winning the Ice Bowl

"If you'll not settle for anything less than your
best, you will be amazed at what you can
accomplish in your lives."

~Vince Lombardi

WHO DECIDES THE TEAMS' SCHEDULES?

COMPUTERS ARE USED IN A SECURE ROOM TO HELP DECIDE WHICH TEAMS WILL PLAY EACH OTHER. THIS PROCESS TAKES HUNDREDS OF HOURS, WHICH BEGINS IN JANUARY OF EACH YEAR. THEY ALSO HAVE TO CONSIDER WHICH STADIUMS ARE BEING USED FOR OTHER EVENTS, WHAT THE SURFACE OF THE STADIUM IS LIKE, OTHER CONFLICTS TEAMS MAY HAVE, AND EVEN TRAFFIC FLOW. EVERY TEAM WILL PLAY THE OTHER THREE TEAMS IN THEIR DIVISION TWICE, ONCE AT HOME AND ONCE AWAY.

IN ADDITION, EACH TEAM PLAYS ONE GAME AGAINST EACH OF THE FOUR TEAMS FROM A DIVISION WITHIN ITS CONFERENCE-

TWO GAMES AT HOME AND TWO ON THE ROAD. WHICH DIVISION A TEAM PLAYS IS DECIDED BY A ROTATION SYSTEM TO MAKE SURE THAT THE TEAMS IN ONE DIVISION WILL PLAY THE TEAMS IN EVERY OTHER DIVISION IN ITS CONFERENCE ONCE EVERY THREE YEARS.

EACH NFL TEAM PLAYS 16 GAMES OVER A 17-WEEK PERIOD. THE NFL USES A FORMULA ON A COMPUTER TO DECIDE ALL 256 MATCHUPS.

CHAPTER 6
MORE ABOUT VINCE

Vince Lombardi was known for being moody and having a temper. Some players thought he was selfish while others thought he was very giving. One thing is for sure, Vince knew football. He was a master at working out football plays in his head and he really enjoyed solving difficult problems related to football.

Vince was also a deeply religious man. When he saw a priest or a nun, he went out of his way to greet them and often gave them free tickets to the games. He also went to Catholic mass every day and regularly went to confession. He also encouraged his players to practice religion but didn't force his on them.

Vince attended daily mass at this Green Bay church

Vince put a lot of pressure on himself to be perfect. He expected his players to be professional. Players must consider how they dressed, where they went out to eat, and how they behaved. He often said, "Confidence is contagious. So is lack of confidence." He felt that if someone had talent they had better use it. Not to use talent was a waste in his mind.

Lombardi believed there were leaders and there were followers, and that those that were followers had better learn to follow and make the world a simpler place.

Competition was important to Vince. He believed that it was the core of high school and college sports. To win, a person must have fire inside of them at the time of the competition. It helped to win games. Lombardi knew what it took to motivate his players to maximize their performance.

Detroit Lions and Chicago Bears were at the top of Vince's list for teams to dislike. He urged his players to dislike those teams as well. The only team that Vince didn't want his players to dislike was Vince's old team, the New York Giants. Vince always had a soft spot for that team, even if he did want to beat them on game day.

Following rules also mattered to Vince, especially on the football field. He never wanted his players to have unsportsmanlike behavior on or off the field. As a coach he also believed in following the rules and rarely did he break them during a game. He did, however, once follow an official into a dressing room to tell him how upset he was with the call made. This was against NFL rules but rather than give Vince a fine, the NFL commissioner sent him a letter telling him how wrong Vince's behavior was. Vince felt bad and apologized.

Vince was an excellent motivator. How he did that depended on his mood at the time and the player he was dealing with. Vince said that his teaching background was what really helped him to be a good coach. Being a good teacher was how he taught his players to become excellent players. "They call it coaching but it is teaching. You do not just tell them...you show them the reasons." Lombardi used rote (repeating over and over again) to help his players to learn the plays and moves he wanted them to use during the game. He also knew that practice could not get boring, so he planned his practices with just enough differences to keep the players' minds sharp and interested in learning.

Thursday, Friday, and Saturday before a game, Vince sat down with his quarterbacks to go over the strategy. He wanted to be sure they were prepared to handle any situation that may come up during the game. Quarterbacks could call the plays while on the field during a game and Vince rarely talked with them at that time. He had a lot of confidence in his players, especially Bart Starr, to remember the plays and know when to use them. He also didn't believe in changing the plan during game time. Vince had his players doing what every other team was doing, the Packers just did it better.

The running game was what Vince was most comfortable with. Rather than having his players pass the ball, they ran with it. He knew they could get the ball to move this way. He liked it because it took all eleven players to be successful, and he could practice it and polish it with his team. It also allowed his players to attack where the opponent went.

Watching films of old games and of other teams was another way Vince helped the Packers become winners. After a game, Vince had his players watch it over again. Many players dreaded this because Vince pointed out every little mistake that was made. Those mistakes would be worked on and fixed in time for the next game. Lombardi knew most teams were pretty even in regard to the talent and pay, so he had to use motivation to make the difference in whether his team won or lost. To do this, he sometimes criticized, nagged, or even threatened his players to do what he wanted. At other times, Lombardi was charming, kind, and caring. The team never knew which way Vince was going to react.

During the 1960s, when Vince was coaching the Packers, racism (the belief that some people are better than others, often because of skin color or race) was an issue with many teams. African American players were often told they had to bunk only with other African American players. When the Packers traveled to North Carolina for an exhibition game, four African American players were not allowed to stay with the rest of the team at the hotel. They were told they had to stay at the dorms at a nearby university. This made Vince angry and he promised his players that they would never travel to places unless all players were treated respectfully and equally. Another time, the African American players were told to come and go through the back door of a restaurant. Vince decided that all of his players would use the back door. He felt that discrimination was terrible. Vince knew how it felt to be discriminated against and teased because he was Italian. Lombardi believed that the Packers were a family. In fact, they were thought of as the most family-like team in the entire NFL. Players fought to come to Green Bay to play and never wanted to leave. Vince also hated to see players leave Green Bay. Sometimes due age, injury, or trade he'd have to tell a player that his time was over with the Packers. Those were hard conversations for him to have because he cared for his players and their families, even feeding them at his home every Thanksgiving. It got so hard for Vince to say goodbye to players that he gave the job to another man who worked for the Packers.

Vince expected people to arrive early. For example, if Vince says to meet at 8 AM for breakfast, he expects people to be there at 7:45 AM. So, if you arrive at 7:55 AM, you are ten minutes late. That is what is called "Lombardi Time".

Green Bay had a population of 63,000 people at the time Vince was coach. He was one of the most famous people there, and was often asked to sign autographs, which he hated doing, but he almost never refused a child. He wasn't patient with the local reporters when they wanted to interview him. Many were afraid to ask him a question for fear of his response.

Vince Lombardi is a legend when it comes to coaching. He always tried to inspire others to be the best they could be. His legacy is carried on today in the Lombardi Trophy that is given out to the winner of the Super Bowl each year. It symbolizes greatness, exactly what Vince Lombardi was as a coach.

The Vince Lombardi Trophy that is given to the winning team of the Super Bowl each year

PAUL HARVEY RADIO SHOW

ON THE DAY THAT VINCE LOMBARDI
PASSED AWAY, PAUL HARVEY, ON HIS
RADIO PROGRAM, IS QUOTED AS SAYING, "IT
IS A GRAY DAY IN GREEN BAY, WISCONSIN.
THE HEAVENS ARE WEEPING IN GREEN BAY
BECAUSE VINCE LOMBARDI HAS PASSED
AWAY. HIS TEAM RAN ON LOMBARDI TIME,
15 MINUTES BEFORE EVERYWHERE ELSE.

"Obstacles are what you see when you take
your eyes off the goal."

~Vince Lombardi

Timeline

-1913 VINCENT THOMAS LOMBARDI BORN IN

BROOKLYN, NY

-1921 VINCE BEGINS SCHOOL AT P.S. 206 IN

NEW YORK CITY

-1929 VINCE BEGINS HIGH SCHOOL AT

CATHEDRAL PREP IN BROOKLYN, NEW YORK

-1932 VINCE LEAVES CATHEDRAL PREP AND

DECIDES NOT TO BECOME A PRIEST

-1932 VINCE JOINS ST. FRANCIS ACADEMY

WITH A FOOTBALL SCHOLARSHIP

-1933 VINCE BEGINS COLLEGE AT FORDHAM

UNIVERSITY IN THE BRONX, NY

-1934 VINCE MEETS HIS WIFE MARIE
PLANITZ

-1937 VINCE GRADUATES FROM FORDHAM
UNIVERSITY

-1937-1939 VINCE WORKS ODD JOBS TO MAKE
MONEY WHILE LIVING AT HOME

-1939 VINCE IS HIRED BY ST. CECELIA HIGH
SCHOOL IN ENGELWOOD, NJ

-1947-48 VINCE ACCEPTS AN ASSISTANT
FOOTBALL COACHING POSITION AT
FORDHAM UNIVERSITY

-1948-1954 VINCE TAKES A JOB AS AN
ASSISTANT COACH AT WEST POINT
MILITARY ACADEMY

-1954-1958 VINCE WORKS AS AN OFFENSIVE
COACH FOR THE NEW YORK GIANTS

-1959-1968 VINCE ACCEPTS A HEAD
COACHING POSITION FOR THE GREEN BAY
PACKERS

-1968 VINCE RETIRES FROM COACHING AND
STAYS ON AT GREEN BAY AT THE GENERAL
MANAGER

-1969 VINCE ACCEPTS A HEAD COACHING
POSITION FOR THE WASHINGTON REDSKINS

-1970 VINCE PASSES AWAY FROM CANCER

Bibliography

"1961 Green Bay Packers Starters, Roster, & Players." Pro-Football-Reference.com, www.pro-football-reference.com/teams/gnb/1961_roster.htm.

"Army Black Knights Football." Wikipedia, Wikimedia Foundation, 7 Mar. 2018, en.wikipedia.org/wiki/Army_Black_Knights_football.

"A Brief History of Green Bay." Wisconsin Historical Society, 24 July 2012, www.wisconsinhistory.org/Records/Article/CS2400.

Britannica, The Editors of Encyclopaedia. "Green Bay." Encyclopædia Britannica, Encyclopædia Britannica, Inc., 16 Feb. 2018, www.britannica.com/place/Green-Bay-Wisconsin.

"Creating the NFL Schedule." NFL Football Operations, operations.nfl.com/the-game/creating-the-nfl-schedule.

"Curly Lambeau." Wikipedia, Wikimedia Foundation, 1 Apr. 2018, en.wikipedia.org/wiki/Curly_Lambeau.

DiScipio, Christopher. "7 Things You Didn't Know About Football Helmets." Thrillist, Thrillist, 5 Sept. 2014, www.thrillist.com/gear/a-brief-history-of-nfl-helmets.

Gruver, Ed. "The Lombardi Sweep." The Coffin Corner, 1997, www.profootballresearchers.org/archives/Website_Files/Coffin_Corner/19-05-712.pdf.

"Hall of Famers." News RSS, www.packers.com/history/hall-of-famers/lombardi-vince.html.

History.com Staff. (2009). U.S. Immigration Before 1965. Retrieved January 25, 2018, from http://www.history.com/topics/u-s-immigration-before-1965

History of Green Bay, www.ci.green-bay.wi.us/history/1800s.html.

Julita. "Difference Between." Difference Between Similar Terms and Objects, 3 Jan. 2013, www.differencebetween.net/miscellaneous/difference-between-nfc-and-afc/.

"Lambeau Field." Wikipedia, Wikimedia Foundation, 8 Mar. 2018, en.wikipedia.org/wiki/Lambeau_Field.

Lombardi, Vince, and Gary George. *Winning Is a Habit*. HarperCollins, 1998.

"Milwaukee County Stadium." Wikipedia, Wikimedia Foundation, 6 Mar. 2018, en.wikipedia.org/wiki/Milwaukee_County_Stadium.

"NCAA Division I Football Bowl Subdivision." Wikipedia, Wikimedia Foundation, 6 Mar. 2018, en.wikipedia.org/wiki/NCAA_Division_I_Football_Bowl_Subdivision.

"NFL Teams - NFL Football Teams by Division." Home - Sports News, Scores, Schedules, and Videos, Fox News, www.foxsports.com/nfl/teams.

O'Brien, M. (1987). *Vince: A Personal Biography of Vince Lombardi*. New York City, NY: William Morrow and Company.

"Packers Beat Chiefs in First Super Bowl." History.com, A&E Television Networks, www.history.com/this-day-in-history/packers-beat-chiefs-in-first-super-bowl.

Pincus, David. "12/31/1967 - The Ice Bowl." SBNation.com, SBNation.com, 31 Dec. 2010, www.sbnation.com/2010/12/31/1059489/12-31-1967-the-ice-bowl.

Roensch, Greg. *Vince Lombardi*. Rosen Central, 2003.

Rothman, Michael, and Lindsey Jacobson. "The Story Behind the First Super Bowl." ABC News, ABC News Network, 5 Feb. 2016, abcnews.go.com/Sports/story-super-bowl/story?id=36689661.

"Super Bowl History." Ticket City, www.ticketcity.com/super-bowl-tickets/super-bowl-history.html.

"Super Bowl II." Wikipedia, Wikimedia Foundation, 3 Mar. 2018, en.wikipedia.org/wiki/Super_Bowl_II.

"TV History." TV Set Prices, www.tvhistory.tv/tv-prices.htm.

"United States Military Academy West Point." West Point Military Academy, West Point Military Academy, www.usma.edu/SitePages/Home.aspx.

Wessels. "Television." Television during the 1950s and 60s, Wessels Living History Farm, livinghistoryfarm.org/farminginthe50s/life_17.html.

YouTube, 6 Feb. 2018, youtu.be/qzcvbBaqkNM.

Zirin, Dave. "Those Nonprofit Packers." The New Yorker, The New Yorker, 19 June 2017, www.newyorker.com/news/sporting-scene/those-non-profit-packers.

Made in the USA
Middletown, DE
13 April 2019